My Science Library

The Amazing Facts About Sound

by Buffy Silverman

Science Content Editor:
Shirley Duke

Rourke
Educational Media

rourkeeducationalmedia.com

Teacher Notes available at
rem4teachers.com

Science Content Editor: Shirley Duke holds a bachelor's degree in biology and a master's degree in education from Austin College in Sherman, Texas. She taught science in Texas at all levels for twenty-five years before starting to write for children. Her science books include *You Can't Wear These Genes, Infections, Infestations, and Diseases, Enterprise STEM, Forces and Motion at Work, Environmental Disasters,* and *Gases.* She continues writing science books and also works as a science content editor.

www.rourkeeducationalmedia.com

Photo credits: Cover © VikaSuh, articular, Artisticco; Pages 2/3 © TDC Photography; Pages 4/5 © stockshot, JinYoung Lee; Pages 6/7 © Dragos Iliescu, Oguz Aral; Pages 8/9 © NatalieJean, Igor Kovalchuk, Brian Becker; Pages 10/11 © Michal Durinik, Christopher Parypa; Pages 12/13 © Gina Smith, Mark Herreid; Pages 14/15 © efirm, Avesun, Willyam Bradberry, CreativeNature.nl, dean bertoncelj, Henrik Larsson; Pages 16/17 © Golden Pixels LLC, Galushko Sergey, TDC Photography; Pages 18/19 © Susan Stevenson , Blue Door Education, Keith Publicover, R. Gino Santa Maria, irin-k, Lars Christensen, mast3r, Adisa, Elnur, Stephen Coburn; Pages 20/21 © SergiyN, Waj

Editor: Kelli Hicks

My Science Library series produced by Blue Door Publishing, Florida for Rourke Educational Media.

Library of Congress PCN Data

Silverman, Buffy.
 The Amazing Facts About Sound / Buffy Silverman.
    p. cm. -- (My Science Library)
 ISBN 978-1-61810-109-9 (Hard cover) (alk. paper)
 ISBN 978-1-61810-242-3 (Soft cover)
 Library of Congress Control Number: 2012930307

Rourke Educational Media
Printed in the United States of America,
North Mankato, Minnesota

rourkeeducationalmedia.com

customerservice@rourkeeducationalmedia.com
PO Box 643328 Vero Beach, Florida 32964

Table of Contents

What is Sound?

Listen to the sounds you hear while riding your bicycle to the park. Your bicycle chain clinks as it turns. Cars honk and tires screech on the street. In the park, birds sing and chipmunks chirp. The wind blows and leaves rustle. A friend shouts your name. Your brakes squeak as you squeeze them to stop. Your bicycle lock clicks in place. Every day you are surrounded by sounds.

We cannot see sound. But sounds impact us every day. We learn about our surroundings by listening to sounds.

Sound is a form of **energy**. Pluck a guitar string and it vibrates, or moves back and forth. The **vibrations** form **sound waves**. Sound waves move through air, water, and solid material. As they travel, they collide with microscopic particles. Sound waves make these particles, called **molecules**, vibrate.

Knock on a door and molecules in the door vibrate. The moving molecules collide with air particles, sending sound waves through the air.

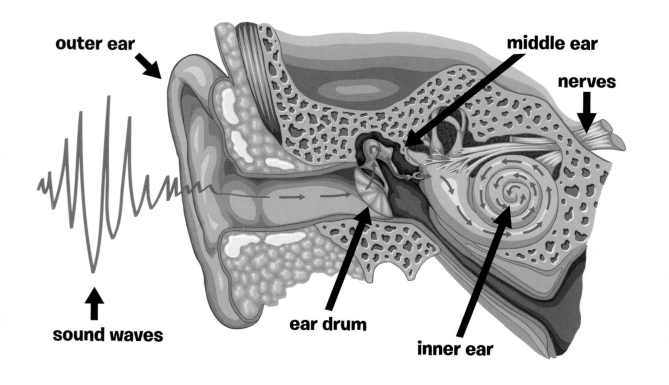

Sound waves in the air are collected by your outer ear. They travel to the **eardrum** and make it vibrate. Then, vibrations pass through bones in the middle ear to the inner ear. They bend tiny hairs in the inner ear, causing nerves to fire that send messages to the brain. Your brain hears sound.

Speeding Sound

●○●○●○●○●○●○●○●○●○●○●○●

Sound can only travel through material, called **matter**. Solids, liquids, and gases like air are all made of matter. The speed of sound is the speed that sound waves travel through matter. Sound travels faster through a solid than a liquid, and faster through a liquid than a gas. Molecules in a solid are packed together so vibrations move rapidly from molecule to molecule. Molecules in a liquid are farther apart. Molecules in a gas are farthest apart so vibrations travel slowest.

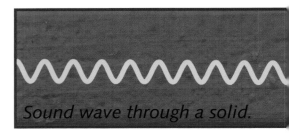

Sound wave through a solid.

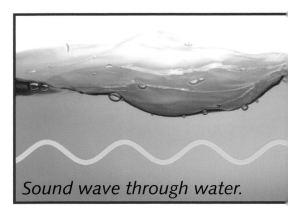

Sound wave through water.

Sound wave through air.

Amazing Sound Fact

The sound of stomping elephant feet travels many times faster through the ground than through the air. Elephants detect these vibrations with their sensitive trunks and feet. They feel vibrations that are two miles (3.22 kilometers) away.

Sea lions hear better under water than on land, because sound waves travel faster through water than air.

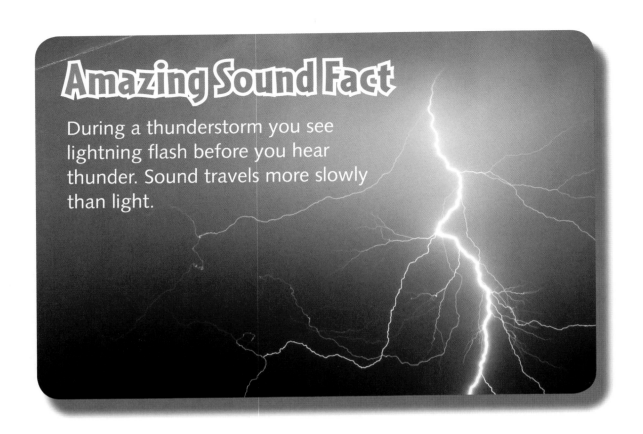

Amazing Sound Fact

During a thunderstorm you see lightning flash before you hear thunder. Sound travels more slowly than light.

Sound travels through 68° Fahrenheit (20°Celsius) air at about 768 miles per hour (1,236 km/hour) at sea level. Molecules have more energy and vibrate faster at higher temperatures so sound travels faster in warmer air. Most airplanes travel slower than the speed of sound. But some jets can break through the sound barrier.

When a jet travels at the speed of sound, known as Mach 1, sound waves press the air in front of the plane. To travel faster than sound, the plane must break through these waves. A speeding jet breaks through these waves, making an explosive sound called a sonic boom.

A cloud of vapor sometimes forms around a jet as it approaches the speed of sound. The lowered air pressure from the plane's lift and disturbed air around it condenses the moisture in the air, causing the vapor cloud.

High or Low?

A mosquito buzzes in your ear, making a high-pitched noise. A tugboat travels through fog, blasting its low-pitched horn. You hear many sounds with different pitches. The **pitch** of a sound depends on how frequently the particles in air vibrate before reaching your ear. A high, squeaky sound causes more vibrations per second. A low, rumbling sound causes fewer vibrations per second.

Musicians in a marching band play high and low-pitched sounds. Flutes make high-pitched sounds. Tubas make low-pitched sounds.

flute

Amazing Sound Fact

The pitch of a sound depends on its frequency. Frequency is defined as the number of sound waves that pass a point each second.

Short wavelength means lots of waves; high frequency means high-pitch sound. ⊢—⊣

⊢————⊣ Long wavelength means fewer waves; low frequency means low-pitch sound.

tuba

A bat makes high-pitched clicks as it flies through the night. You might see a bat as it swoops through the air, but you cannot hear it. Bats and other animals make and hear sounds that people cannot detect.

People hear sounds that vibrate between 20 and 20,000 times in a second. Bats hear sounds that vibrate up to 200,000 times a second. Sounds with a higher frequency than humans can hear are called **ultrasounds**.

Dogs, cats, dolphins, and mice can hear ultrasounds. Certain crickets, moths, and frogs make and hear ultrasounds, too.

Amazing Sound Fact

Bats use a special sense, called **echolocation**. They listen to **echoes** of their ultrasonic calls to find food and avoid obstacles.

bat sonar

returning sound waves

Loud or Soft?

Leaves rustle in a gentle breeze. A jet engine roars as the jet taxis down a runway. Some sounds are soft and others are loud. The amount of energy in a sound, called its intensity, determines how loud it is. Sounds with more intensity cause larger vibrations, which we hear as louder sounds. Tap a table lightly. Your tap makes a small vibration and a soft sound. Now hit the table hard. It vibrates more and makes a louder sound.

Which has more intensity? A whisper or a rock concert?

Amazing Sound Fact

When a drummer beats a drum hard, it makes a large vibration and a loud sound. If the drummer strikes the drum softly, the vibration is smaller and the sound quieter.

Amazing Sound Fact

The amount of energy in a sound wave is measured as its height or **amplitude**. Loud sounds have greater amplitude than soft sounds.

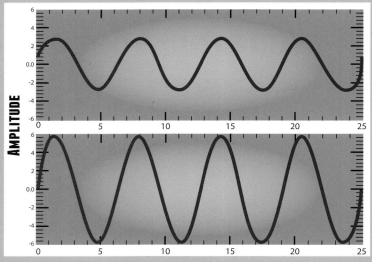

Machines called oscilloscopes measure amplitude. The sound wave at the top of the diagram has less energy and makes a softer sound than the sound wave at the bottom.

People measure the loudness of sound in a scale called **decibels**. Loud sounds that are greater than 85 decibels can damage your hearing. Long exposure to noise can also cause hearing loss. People who work on construction sites, in airports, and other loud places protect their ears by wearing ear protection.

A jackhammer creates a sound of 130 decibels.

18

Typical Sound Levels

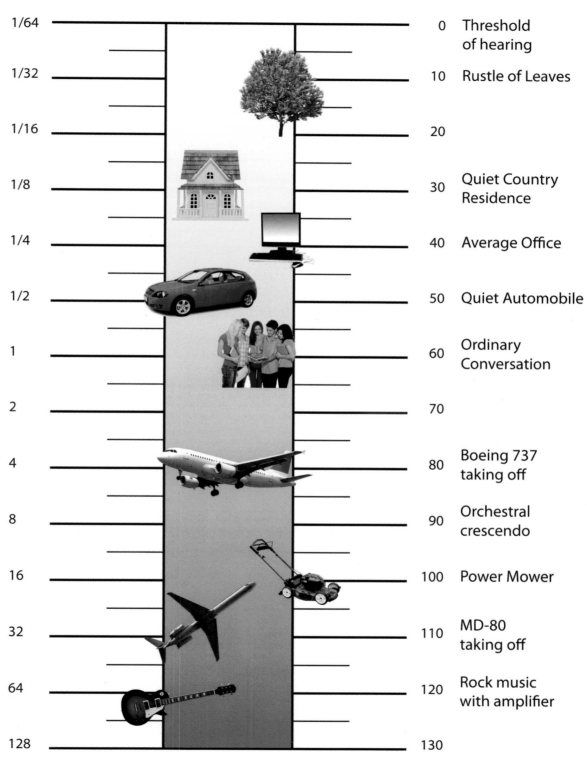

Relative Loudness		Decibels	
1/64		0	Threshold of hearing
1/32		10	Rustle of Leaves
1/16		20	
1/8		30	Quiet Country Residence
1/4		40	Average Office
1/2		50	Quiet Automobile
1		60	Ordinary Conversation
2		70	
4		80	Boeing 737 taking off
8		90	Orchestral crescendo
16		100	Power Mower
32		110	MD-80 taking off
64		120	Rock music with amplifier
128		130	

Relative Loudness

Decibels

19

Sound waves travel in all directions. What happens when a sound wave reaches an obstacle? If a wave reaches a soft, uneven surface, most of the energy is absorbed by it. But if a sound wave hits a hard, smooth surface, the wave is reflected back like light off a mirror. If you yell at a wall that is more than 55 feet (17 meters) away, the sound travels back after you hear the yell. The reflected sound is called an echo.

Architects and engineers build theatres that reflect sound for high quality listening experiences. They want audiences to get the most out of each and every performance.

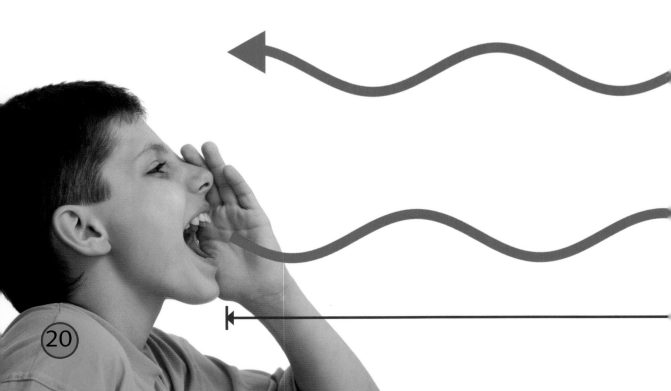

Amphitheaters, both ancient and modern, have a curved shaped to create an area which echoes or amplifies sound.

Much of what you know about the world you learn by listening to sounds. Every day you hear soft and loud sounds. You make high-pitched and low-pitched sounds when you sing and play an instrument. Sound waves bring us information about our world.

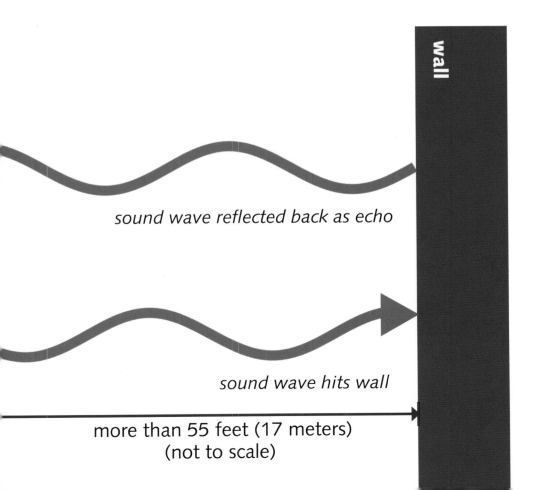

wall

sound wave reflected back as echo

sound wave hits wall

more than 55 feet (17 meters)
(not to scale)

21

Show What You Know

1. What happens to molecules when a sound wave collides with them?

2. How does the sound wave of a high pitch sound differ from the sound wave of a low pitch sound?

3. Why are certain sounds louder than other sounds?

Glossary

amplitude (AM-pluh-tood): the maximum value or height of a wave

decibels (DESS-uh-belz): units for measuring the volume of sounds

eardrum (IHR-drum): part of the middle ear that vibrates when sound waves reach it

echoes (EK-ohz): repetitions of a sound caused by the reflection of a sound wave off a hard, smooth surface

echolocation (EK-oh-loh-KAY-shuhn): process by which bats, dolphins, and other animals find objects by making sounds and listening to their echoes

energy (EN-ur-jee): active or working power, or force needed to do something

matter (MAT-ur): anything that has mass and takes up space

molecules (MAH-luh-kyoolz): the smallest units of a substance that has all the properties of that substance

pitch (PICH): the highness or lowness of a sound, as determined by the rate of vibrations that make the sound

sound waves (SOUND WAVEZ): series of vibrations in a solid, liquid, or gas that can be heard

ultrasounds (UHL-truh-soundz): sounds whose frequency are too high for humans to hear

vibrations (vye-BRA-shunz): rapid back and forth movements

Index

Websites to Visit

http://www.grc.nasa.gov/WWW/k-12/airplane/sndwave.html
http://www.questacon.edu.au/activities/musical_coathanger.html
http://www.wildmusic.org/

About the Author

Buffy Silverman likes listening to snow crunch in winter, birds sing in spring, bullfrogs call in summer, and leaves swirl in autumn. When she's not exploring the great outdoors, she writes about science and nature.

Ask The Author!
www.rem4students.com